W9-AVD-297

SCIENCE AROUND US

Mollusks and Crustaceans

By Peter Murray

THE CHILD'S WORLD®
CHANHASSEN, MINNESOTA

Published in the United States of America by The Child's World®
PO Box 326, Chanhassen, MN 55317-0326
800-599-READ
www.childsworld.com

Content Advisers:
Jim Rising, PhD,
Professor of Zoology,
University of Toronto,
Department of Zoology,
Toronto, Ontario,
Canada, and Trudy
Rising, Educational
Consultant, Toronto,
Ontario, Canada

The Child's World®: Mary Berendes, Publishing Director

Editorial Directions, Inc.: E. Russell Primm, Editorial Director; Pam Rosenberg, Line
Editor; Katie Marsico, Assistant Editor; Matt Messbarger, Editorial Assistant; Susan
Hindman, Copy Editor; Susan Ashley, Proofreader; Peter Garnham, Terry Johnson,
Olivia Nellums, Katherine Trickle, and Stephen Carl Wender, Fact Checkers; Tim
Griffin/IndexServ, Indexer; Cian Loughlin O'Day, Photo Researcher; Linda S. Koutris,
Photo Selector

The Design Lab: Kathleen Petelinsek, Design and Page Production

Library of Congress Cataloging-in-Publication Data
Murray, Peter, 1952 Sept. 29–
  Mollusks and crustaceans / by Peter Murray.
      p. cm. — (Science around us)
  Includes index.
  ISBN 1-59296-217-3 (library bound : alk. paper) 1. Mollusks—Juvenile literature.
2. Crustacea—Juvenile literature. I. Title. II. Science around us (Child's World (Firm))
  QL405.2.M87 2004
  594—dc22   2004003646

TABLE OF CONTENTS

CHAPTER ONE

SEAFOOD PLATTER, ANYONE?

When most people think of mollusks and crustaceans, they think "seafood." Shellfish such as lobsters, oysters, clams, and crabs are all mollusks or crustaceans. But mollusks and crustaceans are not at all closely related. They are more different from one

Some mollusks and crustaceans are often eaten by humans as part of a seafood platter.

another than birds are from fish.

Long before the first creatures

crawled onto dry land, the oceans

were filled with soft, squishy life

forms: bacteria, **plankton,** and

jellyfish were tossed about by the

currents. Sponges clung to the

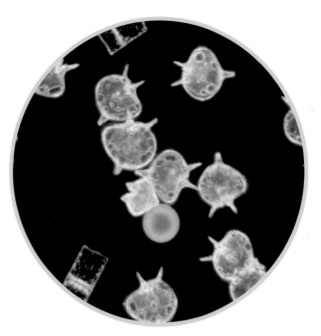

Plankton are tiny living things that float in the oceans and are eaten by many larger animals.

rocky ocean bottoms. Early kinds of worms wriggled in the muck.

Little changed for hundreds of millions of years.

Then, about 550 million years ago, a new kind of creature

emerged—the first mollusks. Like roundworms, mollusks had heads

and tails, one-way digestive systems, and muscles that could move

them across the ocean floor. But they also had something new: a

hard, protective shell. These first mollusks were the original shellfish.

CHAPTER TWO

WHAT IS A MOLLUSK?

What does a garden snail have in common with an 18-meter-long (60-foot-long) giant squid? They are both mollusks. Clams, slugs, scallops, cuttlefish, and octopuses are mollusks, too. There are about 100,000 **species** of mollusks. Most of them live in the water—only some snail and slug species live on dry land. But what makes a mollusk a mollusk?

Nudibranches, or sea slugs, are mollusks that do not have shells. Some of them are brightly colored.

A moon snail feeds on kelp, or seaweed.

Seashells are the remains of long-dead mollusks.

The first thing you notice about most mollusks is their hard protective shell. Clams and oysters can shut themselves completely in their shells. Sea snails grow shells in a wide variety of shapes and sizes. Squid and cuttlefish do not have external shells—their shells grow inside their bodies.

The mollusk's shell is attached to its mantle—a layer of tough tissue that protects its heart, digestive system, reproductive organs,

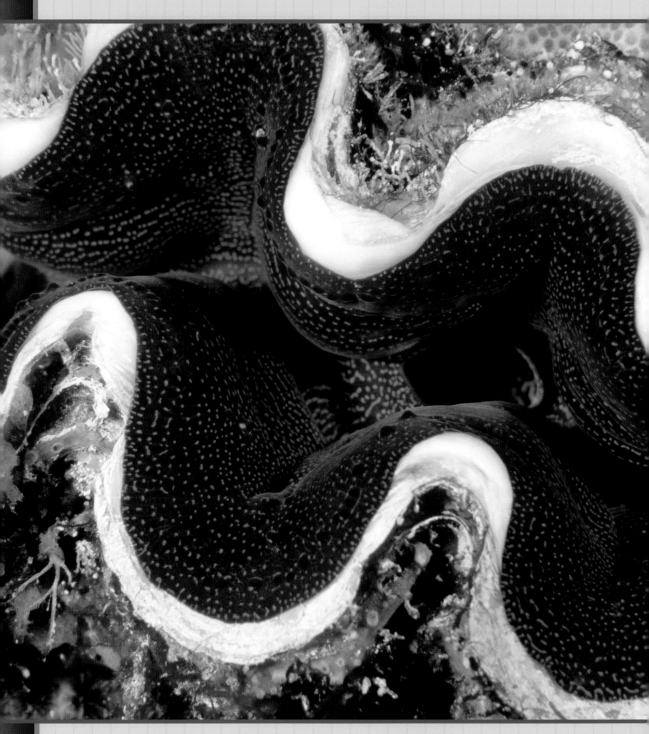

The mantle of this fluted giant clam is blue.

and gills or lungs, depending on where they live. In most species, the mantle **secretes** a substance called calcium carbonate, which hardens to become a shell.

A Spanish dancer sea slug feeds on coral.

Mollusks also have a large, muscular "foot." A clam may use its foot to dig in the sand. A snail uses its foot to crawl along on a trail of slime. The octopus's foot has evolved into eight powerful tentacles.

Most mollusks have a special organ called a radula. The radula is a tongue covered with thousands of tiny teeth. It is used to scrape and grind up food.

Not all mollusks have a mantle, shell, radula, and foot, but they all have at least one of those features.

CHAPTER THREE

TYPES OF MOLLUSKS

BIVALVES

This group of mollusks includes clams, oysters, scallops, and mussels. There are more than 15,000 known bivalve species.

A bivalve has a hinged shell that can open and close. It opens its shell to eat and breathe, but anytime it senses danger, its shell clamps

The mantle of a magnificent scallop (above) is orange. If you look closely, you can see tiny blue dots. These are the scallop's eyes.

Oysters live in colonies such as this oyster bed in a salt marsh in Georgia.

shut. The bivalve shell seals so tightly that clams and oysters can survive for weeks out of the water.

Many bivalves spend their lives either partially buried in the sand or permanently attached to hard surfaces. Mussels and oysters live in colonies with hundreds or thousands of others. Mussels use small hairlike threads to attach themselves to roots, rocks, or other shellfish. Oysters cement themselves to rocks.

Scallops are the only bivalves that can "swim." When threatened,

a scallop snaps its shell shut and shoots out a spurt of water. This

action propels the scallop across the ocean

floor.

Weighing as much as 230 kilograms (500 pounds), the giant clam is the largest of all bivalves.

Scallops, such as this giant rock scallop, are the only bivalves that can swim.

GASTROPODS

With more than 75,000 species, gastropods are the most numerous of the mollusks. They range in size from the tiny garden slug to the 75-centimeter-long (30-inch-long) trumpet conch. Other types of gastropods include land snails, sea slugs, abalones, winkles, cowries, and cone shells. The most beautiful seashells are the remains of dead gastropods.

Gastropods are a favorite food for many people. Conch chowder and abalone steaks are popular with seafood lovers. Land snails are a

> The cone shell hunts by injecting venom into its prey with a hollow, harpoonlike "tongue." It also uses its venom for self-defense and can cause a painful sting.

favorite food in France, where they are called escargot (es-kar-GO).

CEPHALOPODS

The cephalopod class includes octopuses, squid, cuttlefish, and nautiluses. They are the biggest and smartest mollusks.

Most cephalopods have eight arms, a radula, a sharp birdlike beak, and excellent eyesight. They also have a unique defense—when threatened, they can shoot out a blinding cloud of dark ink.

The largest cephalopod—and the largest mollusk of them all—is the giant squid, which can grow to be about 18 meters (60 feet) long and weigh up to 900 kilograms (2,000 pounds). Giant squid live deep in the ocean—no one knows exactly where, and no one has ever seen one alive. We know about them because dead giant squids sometimes wash up onshore, and their beaks have been found in the stomachs of sperm whales.

Squid and cuttlefish have a shell underneath their skin for support. The only cephalopods with no shell at all are the octopuses.

Octopuses are the most intelligent cephalopods. The giant Pacific

When threatened, the cuttlefish squirts out ink which clouds the water and confuses its predators.

octopus grows up to 8 meters (25 feet) long and weighs as much as 270

kilograms (600 pounds). Large octopuses look fearsome, but they are

shy creatures and swim away at any sign of danger.

The only octopus that is dangerous to humans is the blue-ringed

octopus. This tiny octopus measures only about 8 centimeters (3 inch-

es) long, but its bite is poisonous and deadly.

Cuttlefish were once hunted for their ink, which was used for writing and drawing.

The bite of the poisonous blue-ringed octopus can be deadly to humans.

If a chiton (above) is dislodged from the rock it is grazing on, it will curl itself into a ball to protect itself.

OTHER MOLLUSKS

Other types of mollusks include chitons and tusk shells. Chitons have suckerlike feet and eight hard plates protecting their backs. They spend their lives crawling slowly over underwater rocks grazing on **algae.** Tusk shells are **burrowing** mollusks named for their long, tusk-shaped shells.

CHAPTER FOUR

What Is a Crustacean?

Crustaceans—lobsters, shrimp, and crabs—are often grouped together with mollusks as shellfish. But a closer look shows that crustacean bodies do not resemble mollusks at all. They are more closely related to spiders and insects.

Spiny lobsters must shed their exoskeletons, or shells, in order to grow. They do this several times a year when they are young and once a year when they are adults.

Water fleas, or daphnia, are microscopic crustaceans.

Crustaceans are arthropods, the animal group that includes insects, scorpions, spiders, and centipedes. There are more than 40,000 species of crustaceans—from the Japanese spider crab, with its 4-meter (12-foot) leg span, to water fleas so small you need a microscope to see them. But all crustaceans have certain things in common: ten jointed limbs, four antennae, jaws, and an **exoskeleton** made of **chitin.**

CHAPTER FIVE

TYPES OF CRUSTACEANS

LOBSTERS, SHRIMP, AND CRABS

These tasty crustaceans are familiar to everyone who loves

seafood. Some species of lobsters and crabs can grow to be

The blood of the Atlantic lobster is colorless.

20

Gold shrimp are just one of about 2,000 different kinds of shrimp found in the world's oceans, lakes, and streams.

very large—imagine trying to eat a 23-kilogram (50-pound) lobster

or a crab with legs nearly 2 meters

(6 feet) long!

The American lobster feeds on

other crustaceans, fish, and mollusks—

whatever it can grab and crush with its

powerful claws.

Most shrimp are filter feeders—

they use their legs to grab plankton

What's the difference between mollusks and crustaceans? Mollusks usually have a single shell; crustaceans have a complex shell made of several parts. Most mollusks have a radula; crustaceans have jaws. Mollusks have a single foot or several tentacles; crustaceans have several jointed limbs. Most mollusk shells are made of rock-hard calcium carbonate; crustacean shells are made of flexible chitin.

Krill—tiny shrimp less than 3 centimeters (1 inch) long—gather in huge swarms in the southern oceans. They are the most important food for the blue whale, the largest animal on earth.

from the water. Mantis shrimp are bottom dwellers that prey on clams and other mollusks by smashing them with their clublike front limbs.

Most crustaceans never leave the water, but some tropic crabs spend part of their lives on land. They must return to the water to mate and lay eggs. Crabs eat a wide variety of foods. Some species filter plankton from sand and water. Others scrape algae from rocks or search for dead fish on sandy beaches. The robber crab of the South Pacific eats coconuts—it will even climb coconut trees to get them!

BARNACLES

Barnacles look more like mollusks than crustaceans. A barnacle attaches itself to just about anything solid—a rock, a ship's hull, or a whale's hide. It then grows a rock-hard, cone-shaped shell. The bar-

nacle feeds by sticking its feathery feet out the top of its shell and

grabbing tiny food particles from the water.

A goose barnacle uses its feathery feet, called cirri, to trap food.

BRANCHIOPODS AND COPEPODS

Most branchiopods and copepods are so small that you might never notice them. These tiny crustaceans are found wherever there is water—you might think of them as the mosquitoes, flies, and gnats of the sea. Branchiopods and copepods are a major part of plankton, making them an important source of food for fish, mollusks, and larger crustaceans.

Water fleas and brine shrimp are branchiopods. Water fleas live in freshwater ponds and streams. Brine shrimp live in saltwater ponds and lakes. When a pond dries up, the shrimp die, but their eggs can survive for months or years. When rain fills the pond again, it will soon swarm with tiny brine shrimp.

Copepods are tiny, free-swimming crustaceans related to barnacles. They are usually less than $^1/_2$ centimeter ($^1/_4$ inch) long

A pill bug will roll itself up into a ball when it is threatened.

and are found in both freshwater and salt water. Many copepods,

such as fish lice, are parasitic.

PILL BUGS

Pill bugs—also known as wood lice or roly-polies—are the only

crustaceans that live entirely on land. They are common in damp

basements, under logs, and in other moist, shady places.

◆ ◆ ◆

Clams and other mollusks are among the favorite foods of many people.

Centipedes need a moist environment in order to survive.

The next time you order a seafood platter at your favorite restaurant, go to a clambake on the beach, or sit down to a plate of escargot at a fancy French restaurant, try to identify the different mollusks and crustaceans. Think about how they lived, and remember that mollusks and crustaceans are an important part of our planet's ecosystems.

Centipedes and millipedes are not true crustaceans, but they are closely related. Centipedes are fast-moving hunters with one pair of legs per body segment and a poisonous bite. Millipedes have two pairs of legs per segment. They move slowly, feeding on rotting vegetation.

Centipedes and millipedes have been around for hundreds of millions of years. They were among the first animals to live on dry land.

27

GLOSSARY

algae (AL-jee) Algae are small plants that do not have roots or stems. They grow in water or on damp surfaces.

burrowing (BUR-oh-ing) Burrowing is the process of digging underground tunnels or holes that can be used for shelter. A burrowing animal lives in the tunnels or holes it digs.

chitin (KYE-ten) Chitin is the hard, clear substance that forms a shell, or exoskeleton, around a crustacean's body.

exoskeleton (eks-oh-SKEL-uh-tuhn) An exoskeleton is a hard, protective covering on the body of an animal, such as the shell of a lobster.

plankton (PLANGK-tun) The collection of tiny, often microscopic, plants and animals that float or drift in freshwater or salt water is known as plankton.

prey (PRAY) An animal that is hunted by another animal for food is called prey.

secretes (sih-KREETS) If an animal secretes, it produces and gives off a substance, usually in the form of a liquid.

species (SPEE-sheez) A species is a certain type of living thing. Animals of the same species can mate and produce young. Animals of different species cannot produce young together.

vegetation (vej-uh-TAY-shuhn) Vegetation is all of the plants that cover an area.

DID YOU KNOW?

▶ Slugs have lost their shells but they still have a mantle.

▶ The giant African land snail can be up to 30 centimeters (12 inches) long.

▶ A hermit crab doesn't grow a protective shell over its abdomen. Instead, it wedges its soft body into the empty shell of a dead mollusk. When it grows too big for the shell, it leaves and finds a bigger one.

▶ Plankton is made up of thousands of different types of living things, including many crustaceans.

▶ Some scallops have hundreds of bright blue eyes that line the edge of their shells.

▶ Horseshoe crabs are not true crabs. They are more closely related to spiders and scorpions.

▶ Crayfish look like lobsters, but they are much smaller. They live in freshwater lakes and streams.

Hermit crabs can be found all over the world.

29

THE ANIMAL KINGDOM

VERTEBRATES

fish

amphibians

reptiles

birds

mammals

INVERTEBRATES

sponges

worms

insects

spiders & scorpions

mollusks & crustaceans

sea stars

sea jellies

HOW TO LEARN MORE ABOUT MOLLUSKS AND CRUSTACEANS

At the Library

Blaxland, Beth. *Snails, Clams, and Their Relatives: Mollusks.*
Philadelphia: Chelsea House Publishers, 2003.

Fredericks, Anthony D., and Gerry Ellis (photographer).
Slugs. Minneapolis: Lerner Publications, 2000.

Pascoe, Elaine, and Dwight Kuhn (photographer).
Pill Bugs and Sow Bugs and Other Crustaceans.
Woodbridge, Conn.: Blackbirch Press, 2001.

On the Web

VISIT OUR HOME PAGE FOR LOTS OF LINKS ABOUT
MOLLUSKS AND CRUSTACEANS:
http://www.childsworld.com/links.html

Note to Parents, Teachers, and Librarians: We routinely check our Web links to
make sure they're safe, active sites—so encourage your readers to check them out!

Places to Visit or Contact

NATURAL HISTORY MUSEUM OF LOS ANGELES COUNTY
*To tour the Marine Hall and learn more about
mollusks, crustaceans, and other marine animals*
900 Exposition Boulevard
Los Angeles, CA 90007
213/763-3466

THE NORTH CAROLINA AQUARIUM AT FORT FISHER
To learn more about mollusks, crustaceans, and other sea creatures
900 Loggerhead Road
Kure Beach, NC 28449
866/301-3476

INDEX

About the Author

Peter Murray has written more than 80 children's books on science, nature, history, and other topics. An animal lover, Pete lives in Golden Valley, Minnesota, in a house with one woman, two poodles, several dozen spiders, thousands of microscopic dust mites, and an occasional mouse.